Ultimate Cars

JAGUAR

A.T. McKenna

ABDO Publishing Company

Jaguar Sports Cars

For more than 60 years, Britain's prestigious sports car, the Jaguar, has symbolized speed, style, and class. William Lyons and William Walmsley founded the company in 1922. It started as a motorcycle sidecar business in Blackpool, England, and evolved into car making. In 1928, the company moved to Coventry, England, the headquarters for British automobile manufacturing.

The first Jaguar car debuted in 1935. During its first year of production in 1936, about 300 were sold. Then Jaguar went on to make the famous E-types, Mark IIs, and the XK and XJ series.

The Jaguar is a sports car. A sports car is a fast car with a sporty look. It is designed for the fun of driving. Sports cars most often have only two seats. Many times the word *sport* is used in the name of the car. In England sports cars are called roadsters.

Jaguar's logo is a silver, leaping jaguar. It is found on the hood of some Jaguar cars. It is called a hood ornament.

Sir William Lyons

William Lyons was born on September 4, 1901, in England. By the time he was 21 years old, he was co-founder of the Swallow Sidecar Company, which manufactured motorcycle sidecars. Lyons's partner in the sidecar company was William Walmsley.

In 1927, Lyons and Walmsley bought an Austin 7 chassis and built their first car. The chassis is the frame of the car. It looks like the car's skeleton. Their first car was called the Austin Swallow. The first order was for 500 cars!

An Austin Swallow

In 1931, the company introduced the S.S.1. It was an immediate sensation. The S.S. Jaguar sedans and the S.S. 100 sports cars followed.

Lyons and Walmsley sold the sidecar business and started to concentrate on cars. They named their car company Jaguar Cars, Ltd. Then, Walmsley retired and left the company in Lyons's hands.

In 1956, Lyons was knighted. His new title was Sir William Lyons. During the 1950s and 1960s, Lyons acquired several other companies, including Daimler, Guy Motors, and Henry Meadows, Ltd. He also acquired Coventry Climax, which was famous for its racing engines.

In 1968, Lyons joined Jaguar Cars, Ltd. with Sir George Harriman of British Motor Corporation to form British Motor Holdings. Another company called Leyland joined British Motor Holdings, which was renamed British Leyland.

Sir William Lyons retired from the company in 1972. He had run the company for almost 50 years.

In 1984, Jaguar Cars, Ltd. broke away from British Leyland and was headed by John Egan. Egan often looked to Lyons for advice on running the company. Sir William Lyons died in February of 1985.

Famous People in Jaguar History

There are many people at Jaguar who helped build Jaguar sports cars. Sir William Lyons and his partner William Walmsley were the men who started it all with their sidecar business in 1922. When the company expanded in 1934, Walmsley resigned from the partnership, leaving Lyons to head the company.

Malcolm Sayer was a member of the styling, or design, department. He was able to calculate the aerodynamic effects of various car shapes mathematically, decades before Computer Aided Design (CAD) had been invented. Sayer designed the famous E-type cars.

"Lofty" England joined Jaguar as a service manager. He earned his nickname because of his height—6 feet 5 inches (1.95 m). England became managing director of the company in 1968, replacing Sir William Lyons.

Bill Heynes was chief of engineering from 1935 until his retirement in 1969. He worked on many of the Jaguar engine designs, including the XK 6-cylinder engine. This engine was designed by Heynes and his engineering crew on

Sir William Lyons

An XK120 engine

the roof of the Jaguar factory in Coventry, England, during World War II while they were on fire-watch duty.

Walter Hassan was an engine designer who worked with Heynes. Hassan used to work for Bentley Car Company. He joined Jaguar in 1938 and retired in 1972. He helped design the XK engine.

Claude Bailey was also an XK engine designer. Hassan and Bailey designed two lightweight vehicles during World War II.

Harry Weslake was England's greatest expert on cylinder head design. The cylinder head is a big block of metal that seals the top of the cylinders. The cylinders are where the engine burns fuel, which is a mixture of gasoline and air. Weslake's designs increased the Jaguar's horsepower. Horsepower is the amount of power the engine has.

Norman Dewis was chief factory test driver. He drove the different models and gave a report on their performance.

John Egan took over Jaguar in 1980 during a time of great financial trouble. Egan was able to save the troubled company, and in 1986 he was knighted for his efforts. Egan retired from Jaguar in 1990.

The crew at Jaguar worked hard to produce well-performing cars, such as the XK120.

Creating a Car

William Lyons had a great sense of style and was responsible for the cat-like character of the Jaguar. He was involved in the designing of all of the Jaguar cars. He wanted his cars to have a certain look—like a cat!

Lyons knew that building a car takes many people, from designers and engineers to mechanics. Malcolm Sayer was Jaguar's head designer. The designer must come up with an idea of how the car should look. The designer usually draws several versions of the car before it is accepted. Sayer didn't draw small model designs on paper. Instead he drew the cars at full size on long rolls of paper or just on a long wall!

Designers then make clay models of their designs. They use wood and foam to make a frame. Then, warm clay is laid over the frame and allowed to cool. This makes a life-sized model of the car. The model is then painted so it looks like the actual car

Today, computers are often used to design cars. Automobile designers use Computer Aided Design (CAD)

techniques. Once the basic shape of the car is decided, the clay model is scanned into the computer. Then, the designer can change the design with the touch of a button.

The design of the car must be approved by the executives of the company. Once it is approved, the engineers work with the mechanics to build a prototype.

A prototype is a very early version of the car. All the parts on the prototype are tested for strength and quality. Norman Dewis was Jaguar's chief factory test driver. He tested all the prototypes on the streets of England and at race tracks nearby. Protoypes are also displayed at car shows to get people's responses before the actual cars are produced.

After much research is done on the prototype, executives decide whether or not to build the car. If the car is going to be built, changes are made based on the results of the test driving and the response from people who saw it. Usually, the actual car does not look very much like the prototype.

Next, it is time to build the car for the public. Most cars go through an assembly line when being built. An assembly line is a system used to produce many kinds of products, such as cars. Each worker has a specific job to do. The workers line up in rows and perform their jobs as the car moves down the line. One worker may put in the leather interior, while another installs the wheels.

The assembly line was not what we think of today, with machinery doing a lot of the work. Instead, the Jaguar assembly line was more of a production line. One car is produced at a time. Each engine was assembled separately and then placed in the chassis.

*Opposite page: Workers construct
new cars on a Jaguar assembly line*

Jaguar Timeline

S.S.1

S.S. Jaguar 100

XK120

XK150

E-type

XK8

The Early Cars: S.S.1 and S.S.2

The first Swallow car was called the S.S.1. There were several body variations on the S.S.1 car. The first S.S.1 cars were introduced in October 1931 at the London Motor Show. The S.S.2 was also introduced at the London Motor Show. It was actually an S.S.1 with a shorter chassis.

In building the car, Lyons selected an inexpensive chassis from Standard Motor Company. The S.S.1 was known more for its style than its performance. It was not a fast car.

The two-door S.S.1 had a long hood, flowing fenders, wire wheels and a 16 horsepower engine. This car influenced sports car design for the next 50 years.

The shorter S.S.2 was known as the "little brother" to the S.S.1. It had a nine horsepower engine, so it was slower and more compact. It also cost less than the S.S.1.

The S.S. cars were built from 1931 until 1936. Only a few S.S.1 and S.S.2 cars were built in 1936, at which point the company became known as S.S. Jaguar.

Jaguar S.S.1

The First Car Named Jaguar

The first car to carry the name Jaguar was the S.S. Jaguar 100. Making its introduction in late 1935, this first sports car sold for $1,900. Top speed for this two-seater S.S. was 100 mph (161 km/h). This high speed was very uncommon in the 1930s. The car was successful competing in rallies, hill climbs, and sports car races all over Europe.

Since the S.S. Jaguar 100 was a European car, the driver's seat and steering wheel were on the right side of the car. This was because European drivers drove on the left side of the road. They still do today. Jaguar made some cars with left-side steering wheels to export to the United States.

The car was very stylish in the 1930s. It was extremely low and narrow. It had big, flat headlights, flared fenders, tiny vents all over the hood, and a curved dashboard carrying large instruments. The cars in 1936 and 1937 had wooden frames with metal bodies. But for 1938, the S.S. 100s were made with all-steel bodies.

Only about 300 S.S. 100 cars were built, but many of
these cars are still around today. Those who love old, classic
sports cars collect them and display them at classic car
shows. The S.S. 100 was built from 1936 until 1940.

A 1937 S.S. Jaguar 100

XK Leads the Way

After World War II, Lyons changed the name of the company to Jaguar Cars, Ltd. The initials *SS* had been used during the war to refer to Adolf Hitler's storm troopers, which were called *Schutzstaffel*. Lyons did not want people to think the Jaguar car company had anything to do with Hitler, so he chose the new name.

In 1948, Jaguar introduced the XK120. The XK120 debuted at the London Motor Show. It was an instant hit, capturing all the show's publicity.

The XK120 was named after the six-cylinder XK engine that Heynes and Hassan had developed. The XK120 also received its name because engineers figured it would be able to go 120 mph (193 km/h). In fact, when tested, this car hit 132 mph (212 km/h) with 160 horsepower!

Jaguar built 240 XK120s with aluminum bodies and then switched to steel. The XK120 was built from 1948 until 1953. More than 12,000 were built. Only 600 of those stayed in England. The rest were exported.

The XK120

The XK series of sports car continued with the XK140 in 1954. The XK140 was identical in shape to the XK120, but it was a little more bulky. Most Jaguar cars were being exported to the United States. So, the XK140 had large, full-width chrome bumpers, which were more stylish in America. The engine was improved and the horsepower was up to 190. Only about 8,000 of the XK140s were made.

In 1957, the XK150 was introduced. It was the final model in the XK series. This was the first XK to offer the Jaguar "leaper" hood ornament. The XK150 had a new, sleeker body shape. The engine in this model ran at 210 horsepower, reaching 130 mph (209 km/h). More than 9,000 of the Jaguar XK150s were made.

Opposite page: The XK150

Everyone's Favorite: The E-type

Introduced in 1961, the Jaguar E-type was the fastest and most famous sports car in the world during the 1960s. It was designed by Malcolm Sayer. In 1968, the E-type made its debut at the Geneva Auto Show in Switzerland and then in America at the New York International Auto Show. The E-type was called the XKE in the United States.

There were three series of E-types. The Series I E-type reached a top speed of 151 mph (253 km/h) with a 265 horsepower engine.

The Series I E-type was available as a convertible or coupe. The car cost $5,595. It had an all-steel body. The hood was made of three pieces and had no grille. Instead the car had thin chrome bumpers and beautiful glass-covered headlights. It had a face to remember! The Series I E-types were built until 1969.

The Series II E-types came out in 1969 and lasted only two years. These cars had a similar body style to the earlier cars. Since many Jaguars were imported to the United States, the Series II cars had special features required by the government. For example, the headlights could no longer be glass for safety reasons. Turn signals were made larger and the bumper grew thicker. The Series II was considered a better car than the Series I, with fewer mechanical problems.

Next came the Series III E-type. Outside it looked the same as the other E-types, but the engine inside was quite different! In 1971 the first V-12 engine was installed in the E-type. The number after the V stands for how many cylinders there are in the engine. A V-12 engine is very powerful and heavy. Top speed for the V-12 E-type was 135 mph (217 km/h).

The E-type lasted for 14 years, with 1975 being the last year for production.

Modern Jaguars

After over 60 years, Jaguar is still producing fast, stylish sports cars. Now the company, which started in England, is owned by America's Ford Motor Company. Ford bought the company during a time of financial trouble in 1989. The company still kept the name Jaguar and the three factories in England still make the cars. Ford executives worked hard to help bring Jaguar back to producing fine cars.

In 1994, Jaguar reintroduced the XJ series. These cars included the XJ12, XJ6 and the supercharged XJR. The 1998 XJR looks a lot like the Jaguars of the 1930s. It has a mesh grille, curvy body lines, and the "leaper" hood ornament. At 290 horsepower, it has a top speed of 155 mph (250 km/h). The new car costs $67,400 — certainly a lot more than the early Jaguars!

Jaguar came out with the XK8 in 1996. It was the first new Jaguar sports car model in 30 years. It was also the first Jaguar to have a V-8 engine. The XK8 was considered a successor to the XKE (E-type) and appeared at the Geneva Auto Show. That is the same show at which the E-type debuted 35 years before.

The XK8 body and engine were designed in England. A convertible XK8 came out in 1997. This all-new Jaguar created as much enthusiasm as the E-type did when it came out in 1961.

Some say the XK8 is the ultimate sports car of the 1990s. Always built with the finest parts and full of luxury, Jaguar cars remain some of the top sports cars on the road today.

Jaguar presented its new XK8 at the 1996 Geneva Motor Show. It is powered by a 4.0 litre AJ-v98 engine.

Glossary

aerodynamic - a design that reduces air resistance. It allows cars to travel faster and use fuel more efficiently.

Computer Aided Design (CAD) - computer software that allows a person to design a car by using a computer.

convertible - a car which has a top that can be removed. Convertibles have soft tops or hard tops.

coupe - a coupe is a car which is enclosed with a permanent roof.

debut - the first public appearance.

executive - a person who directs or manages a company's affairs.

export - to send goods, such as cars, to another country for sale.

fender - a mental or plastic guard that protects an automobile's tires.

interior - the inside of a car.

knight - the act of raising someone's rank to the level of knight. Today, a knight is person who receives an honorary title from a king or queen. The title is usually received for outstanding work in a profession.

performance - the way in which a car handles.

publicity - the attention someone or something receives from the public.

rally - an automotive competition that takes place on public roads. Drivers must follow regular traffic rules and maintain a specific speed between check points. The drivers do not know the race's route until right before the race starts.

scan - to pass an electric beam over an image. The beam converts the image to electronic properties, which allows the scanned image to be altered or transferred by a computer.

series - Jaguars that are similar to one another are grouped into what is called a series. A series usually lasts several years. All the cars in the series usually have a similar body shape and style.

sidecar - a sidecar is a small vehicle attached to the side of a motorcycle to carry a passenger.

successor - a person or thing that follows or takes the place or another.

Internet Sites

Jaguar Cars Global Homepage
http://www.jaguar.com

This is the official site of Jaguar Cars, Ltd. It has an excellent section on the history of Jaguar cars, as well as plenty of information about new Jaguars.

Jag-Lovers: The Premier Jaguar Enthusiasts' Web Site
http://www.jag-lovers.org/

This site provides all the information a Jaguar lover could ever want. It has information on specific models, both new and old. It also has a photo album, library, and links to other great Jaguar Web sites.

These sites are subject to change. Go to your favorite search engine and type in "Jaguar" for more sites.

Index